THE RIGHTFUL OWNER

PRAISE FOR THE RIGHTFUL OWNER
Seizing, Occupying, and Accessing the Wealth Promised
By Kiameshea Prewitt

"I loved everything about this book! It's packed with so many resources and practical tools and strategies to help apply what's being explained. Consistent implementation leads to results, and Kiameshea has skillfully integrated opportunities to take action throughout the pages of this powerful manual!

The Rightful Owner is perfect for Christian men and women who are looking for strategies to conquer poverty and limiting beliefs once and for all. They've been saying 'ENOUGH,' and this manual is their blueprint to freedom with God.

One of my favorite lines: 'As the queen of my territory, I learned that I cannot share my nation's sensitive intel with just anyone.' This resonated with me because it was hard to keep exciting things God was doing in my life to myself, but He constantly reminded me that this information was on a need-to-know basis."

— **Ashlee Record**, The Assigned Experience
www.theassigned.com

"The concept of Financial Fraudulence Syndrome (FFS) freed me! It was specially developed and coined by the author to address the cultural, societal, and psychological underpinnings that impact how we view, manage, and even respond to financial success. For me, the introduction of FFS was psychologically freeing, a breakthrough that provided a holistic framework to address the spiritual, emotional, and financial challenges we face when accepting wealth.

The Rightful Owner is for everyone—particularly those whose insecure mindsets, culturally skewed views, and fears drive how they manage money. It's for those of us who have fallen into one of the seven mindsets that kept us in bondage. Free your mind, release the shackles, and align your life with God's plan and purpose! Kiameshea writes with a heart for the people—authentic, vulnerable, and willing to take risks to empower Kingdom people to live out God's promises for our lives. This book is an expression of her heart, and it lightened mine. You'll know that she's writing for the wellness of your heart. At least, that's what I felt!"

— **Qwanquita Wright**, LCSW, Focusing on Self
www.focusingonself.net

"The opening preface, 'What happens when you are the reason your hope is deferred? Not God's timing, not life's circumstances—but you,' struck me profoundly. This was a divine revelation for me, a moment when everything clicked into place. This book serves as God's guidance on how I can gather the spoils from my current battles to uphold the house of the Lord. I experienced a breakthrough from the first sentence. I know this book was birthed to further my deliverance and help me access new territory for the Kingdom of God!

The Rightful Owner is for those called to advance the Kingdom—those destined for greatness but struggling to access the resources God has provided. It reveals how we often defer our own hopes through internal barriers. This book reminds us that we are the gatekeepers of our fulfillment, and each time we hesitate, we stifle the very blessings God yearns to give us. The reflection and application sections are some of my favorite parts.

I am also in awe of God's sovereignty. I am the counselor referenced in this book, and God's timing has allowed me to eat from the fruit the author has produced. This book is an active agent in God's plot twist in my life. I am forever grateful for the author's obedience—it's shifting my life, the lives of many, and advancing the Kingdom of God."

— **Jolona Kinlaw**, LCMHC, LCAS, NCC, I've Overcome Counseling & Consulting Services

www.iovercomeservices.com

These readers experienced profound breakthroughs while reading The Rightful Owner and highly recommend it to anyone seeking financial freedom, spiritual deliverance, and Kingdom authority. Kiameshea Prewitt's powerful book will equip you to break free from limiting beliefs and step boldly into your God-given inheritance.

THE RIGHTFUL OWNER

Seizing, Occupying, and Accessing the Wealth Promised

Kiameshea Prewitt, AFC ®, FBS ®

Key Illustrations by macrovector from Freepik

ISBN: 979-8-9892806-7-4

Library of Congress Control Number:

Published by 120 Publishing House.
20535 NW 2nd Avenue, Suite 204
Miami, FL 33169
www.120publishinghouse.com

Hello There!

I am Kiameshea Prewitt, Financial Behavior Specialist to high-achieving Kingdom women like you, and I have a free training for you that will definitely help you apply the principles in this book and see results right away.

In this welcome training you will learn these three things:

1. **The Purpose of the Book,**
2. **Key Takeaways and Insights, and**
3. **Activation of Ownership Prayer.**

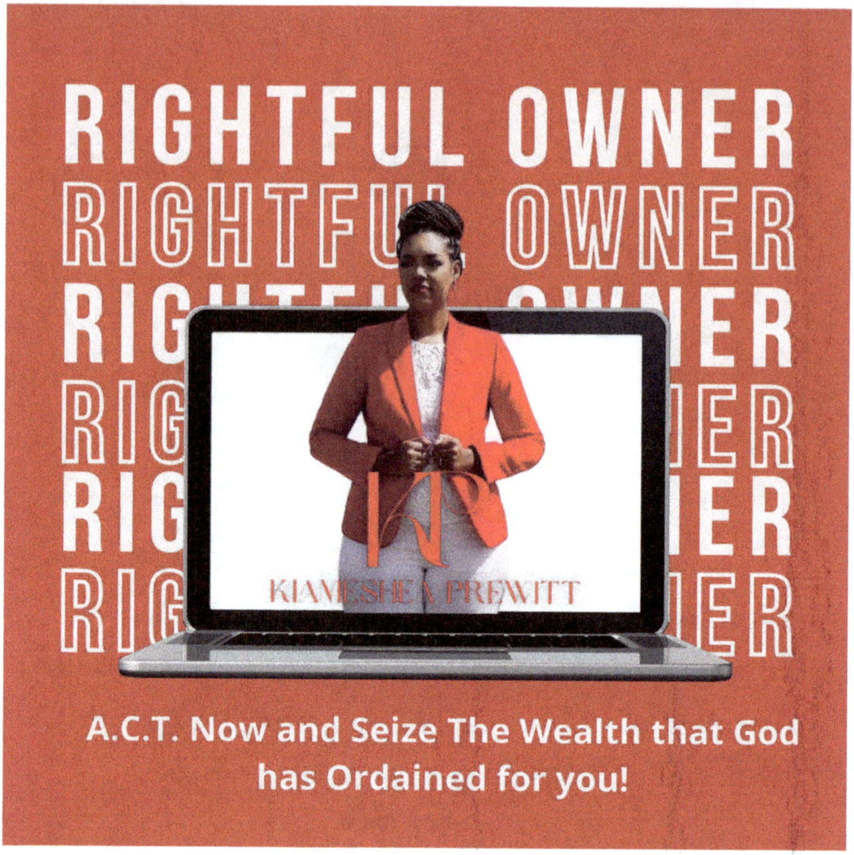

A.C.T. Now and Seize The Wealth that God has Ordained for you!

www.kiamesheaprewitt.com/rightfulowneractivation

I Saved a seat for you!

CAN I LET YOU IN ON A SECRET?

This book you're holding has already made its way into the hands of some truly amazing women—women who, after reading it, began to place a greater demand on my destiny. Their transformative reviews revealed the deep impact of this message, and something extraordinary happened: the program I had planned to release months after the book's launch? I couldn't wait that long. Their breakthroughs inspired me to make it available *now*, in time for you to take full advantage of it as you read.

This book is more than just a collection of pages—it's the starting point of a life-changing journey. And I've created a companion program to help you step fully into what's yours. You'll learn more about it at the end of the book, but since you have this in your hands right now, I wanted to let you in on something special: ***You get exclusive access to my program, Courage to Own.***

This program is designed to go deeper, to help you break free from the limiting beliefs that may still be holding you back from living in your true identity and walking in your God-given purpose. And because you've invested in yourself by getting this book, I want to offer you something extra. You can book a complimentary call with me to reserve your spot in the ***Courage to Own Accelerator*** using a special link just for readers.

This is a unique opportunity to take what you're learning in the book and supercharge it with personalized coaching, spiritual breakthroughs, and the support of a community of like-minded women. Here's a little more about the program:

Courage to Own: A Kingdom Woman's Breakthrough Accelerator

Own Your Identity. Own Your Birthright.
Own Your Assignment.

This program is designed specifically for high-achieving Kingdom women who are ready to break free from limiting beliefs and step boldly into their God-given identity, birthright, and assignment. Through a powerful combination of mindset transformation and actionable breakthroughs, the ***Courage to Own Accelerator*** equips you with the tools to fully claim and own your freedom, purpose, and inheritance.

Excited? I know I am. Book your complimentary call https://bit.ly/CourageCall and let's connect. I'd love to talk not just about your experience with The Rightful Owner but also how this program can help you take the next bold step into your destiny.

Dedication

To the King of kings, my Heavenly Father—thank you for entrusting me with this assignment and for giving me the strength, wisdom, and grace to see it through.

To my husband, Demetris—thank you for believing in me even when I didn't believe in myself. To Makayla and Jace, mommy loves you, and I'm so grateful for your support.

To 120 Publishing, I am thankful that you saw the vision and helped bring it to pass.

And to every reader of this book, may you step boldly into your rightful inheritance and walk in the fullness of the abundant life God has promised.

Contents

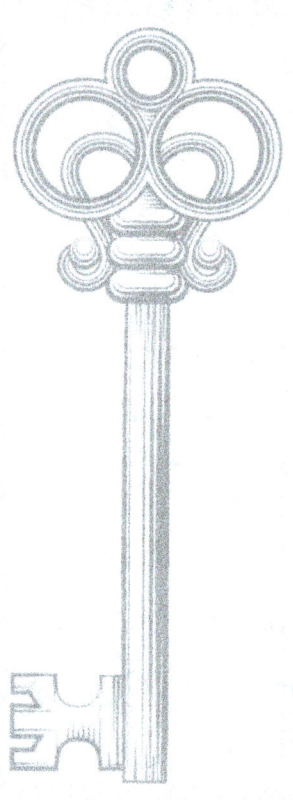

Preface

"Hope deferred makes the heart sick, but a longing fulfilled is a tree of life."
—PROVERBS 13:12

What happens when you are the reason your hope is deferred? Not God's timing, not life's circumstances—**but you**. You are the one blocking the fulfillment of your deepest desires. And to make it even more frustrating, you don't even know what you're doing to stop God from blessing you the way He longs to.

This was my reality for many years. I always sensed I was anointed for more, but no matter how hard I tried, I couldn't figure out how to access the "more." It felt like everyone else—even those who didn't follow God—was able to tap into the overflow. So what was I missing?

Don't misunderstand me—I wasn't in financial despair. God's provision was always there, even when it didn't seem like enough. But I wasn't looking for "just enough." I wanted to experience the *"exceedingly, abundantly above all that we ask or think"* life that the Bible speaks of.

I wanted to know how to unlock the fullness of the promises God had spoken over me. Like Jacob in the Book of Genesis, I knew I was destined for more, and I wasn't willing to settle for less.

For a long time, I was like so many believers—grateful for provision but never bold enough to petition God for the **overflow** that is part of our inheritance. But once you fully grasp who you are in Christ—and, even more importantly, *whose* you are—your spirit will no longer tolerate crumbs.

You've picked up this book because you also know that there's more for you—more than what you've been able to tap into so far. You're no longer willing to let the limitations of this world, the opinions of others, or your own doubts rob you of your rightful inheritance. You've glimpsed, in the spirit, the abundance that has been reserved not only for you but also for your bloodline.

HE DESIRES MORE FOR YOU

Would you believe me if I told you that God desires more for you, too? He is waiting for you to step into everything He has already set aside. You are the treasure He's been waiting for. Even though you've given your life to Him, serve faithfully at church, and perhaps even lead a prayer call or Bible study, **God desires more from you**.

He wants the real, authentic version of you—the one that doesn't hide behind work, motherhood, marriage, or the labels others have placed on you. He wants you to show up fully and unapologetically as the person He designed.

In this book, I'm going to take you on the journey I walked to seize and occupy the abundance God has reserved for me and my bloodline. This journey wasn't easy. It was full of challenges, discouragement, and doubts, but every step was necessary. I'm sharing this with you because there's an urgency on your life as well.

There is a **demand on you**, and it's bigger than just your personal success. You hold the key to unlocking the abundance not just for yourself, but for your entire bloodline. Others before you have faced this calling but didn't rise to the assignment. Will you? Will you reclaim the wealth, influence, and purpose that's been waiting for you?

This book is not just a guide—it's a process. A process that, when followed, will lead you to reclaim the inheritance that has been reserved for you.

Are you ready to take back ownership? This is your time to seize what's yours and walk in the fullness of your Kingdom authority.

Let's begin the journey together.

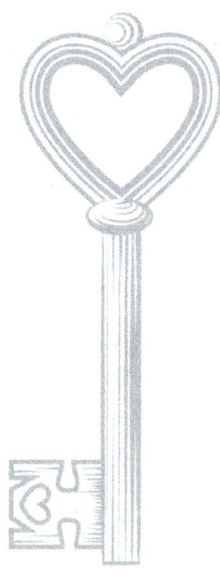

Introduction: How to Use This Book

Welcome to *The Rightful Owner*—a journey into reclaiming your God-given financial inheritance. This book is more than just a collection of stories or spiritual insights; it is a **manual for taking action**. It's a guide that will help you navigate the path from financial uncertainty and lack to **abundance and Kingdom authority**.

Each chapter is designed to awaken you to the spiritual truths behind wealth and ownership, while also providing practical steps for reclaiming your financial destiny. As you move through this book, you'll learn to identify the **7 Unproductive Money Mindsets**, uncover the spiritual battles keeping you from your financial inheritance, and, most importantly, take bold, decisive steps to seize what is rightfully yours.

Here's how to get the most out of this book:

- **Read with Expectation**:
  Every chapter holds revelations that can shift your mindset and unlock breakthrough. Approach each section prayerfully, inviting God to speak to you directly.

- **Engage in the Action Steps**:
  The "Seize the Moment" and "Own It Now" sections at the end of each chapter are designed to move you from reflection to action. Don't skip these steps—these practical exercises are your roadmap to breakthrough.

- **Activate the Anointing**:
  As you read, you will learn how to go deeper into your spiritual authority. Use this book as a tool to actively engage with God and activate your Kingdom calling over your finances.

- **Take Your Time**:
  The principles in this book are powerful, and you may need time to digest and apply them. Don't rush through it—pause, reflect, and act as the Holy Spirit leads.

This is a **living, breathing guide** to stepping into the financial freedom that God has destined for you. As you go through each chapter, keep your heart open to change, your spirit in tune with God, and your actions aligned with His plans for your life.

It's time to take full ownership of your financial destiny.

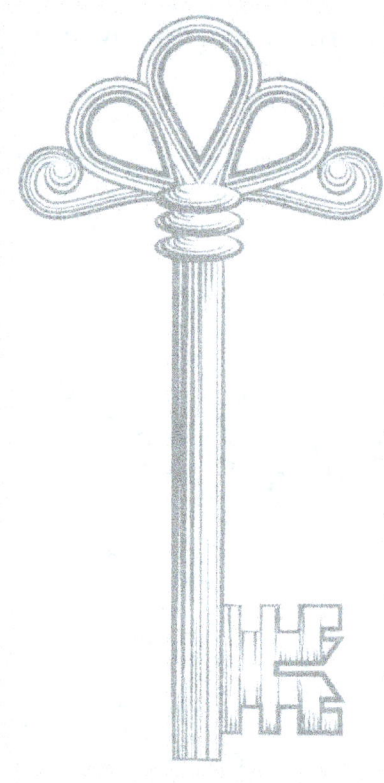

CHAPTER 1:

Living Beneath your privilege

Brigham Young once said, "We live beneath our privileges when we allow worldly anchors to keep us away from the abundant joy that comes from our union with Christ. We live beneath our privileges when we fail to partake of the feast of happiness, peace, and joy that God grants so bountifully to His children." Every time I read this quote, it conjures an image of a young woman standing on the brink of a vast, fruitful land—a realm teeming with riches and boundless opportunities, her rightful inheritance. Yet, despite the beckoning expanse before her, she remains rooted in place, held back not by physical chains, but by heavy, invisible shackles. These shackles are crafted not from iron, but from distorted self-perceptions, societal expectations, and deep-seated personal insecurities. They anchor her to a place of darkness, preventing her from stepping forward to boldly claim the abundant life that is rightfully hers. This woman is vivid in my mind because I was her.

The Awakening: My transformative journey began during a divinely appointed fast, a spiritual practice that stilled the external noise and amplified God's voice. During this sacred time, God didn't just call me to abstain from food; He called me to feast on His Word, specifically on what it says about wealth and the identity of His children. This period of deep reflection and study recalibrated my understanding of prosperity, revealing not only God's perspective on wealth but also how profoundly He values us, His heirs.

The Revelation of Worldly Anchors: The shackles that held me back were composed of various unproductive money mindsets that subtly influenced my life. They formed a barrier between the life I was living and the life God intended for me. As I delved into the scriptures, these anchors were exposed one by one:

1. **Lack of Self-Control:** Often, my spending was impulsive, not covered in prayer or aligned with God's wisdom, leading to regret and unnecessary debt.

2. **Poverty Mindset:** This mindset had me oscillating between needless frugality and excessive spending, misinterpreting what stewardship genuinely entails.

3. **Passive Stewardship:** By neglecting active financial management, I adopted an 'ostrich approach,' burying my head in the sand, avoiding the reality of my finances until crisis struck.

4. **Money is Evil:** Influenced by a misunderstanding of scripture and societal narratives, I believed that wealth could corrupt, failing to see that it is the love of money, not money itself, that is destructive.

5. **Lack of Ownership:** Each financial mishap left me more convinced of my incompetence with money, echoing the enemy's lies that I was unworthy of God's abundance.

6. **False Humility:** Instead of embracing my identity as the head and not the tail, blessed in my comings and goings, I viewed myself through a lens of unworthiness, confusing humility with self-deprecation.

7. **Spirit of Mammon:** I had inadvertently allowed my emotional well-being to become too intertwined with

my financial status, placing an unhealthy emphasis on money.

Embracing the Truth: Imagine this for a moment—your Daddy is the King of Kings. How does that reality sit with you? Does your life reflect this truth, or are there gaps where doubt and fear reside? For me, embracing this fact transformed everything. It wasn't just about acknowledging it as a truth but living it out daily, allowing this identity to seep into every decision, every hope, and every aspiration.

As I confronted each unproductive mindset, replacing lies with truth, the chains began to loosen. The more I aligned my view with God's perspective, the more the anchors lifted, and I could step towards the abundant life that was always intended for me. I realized I was not just meant to survive; I was born to thrive.

Your Call to Action: Now, I extend this revelation to you. You are not meant to live anchored to misconceptions and fears. You are called to live a life of abundance, peace, and joy—an inheritance that your Heavenly Father has laid before you. Let's walk together on this journey of unchaining prosperity, stepping into the fullness of our privileges as children of the Most High King. Are you ready to claim what's rightfully yours and live unanchored by the limitations of this world? Let's step forward boldly, together.

OWN IT NOW:
Stepping into Your Inheritance

In this chapter, we've uncovered the invisible shackles that may be keeping you from fully living out your God-given identity and inheritance. Now it's time to take practical steps toward breaking free from these anchors and embracing the abundance that's already yours.

REFLECTION QUESTIONS:

1. *Identify Your Anchors:* Reflect on the seven unproductive mindsets listed in this chapter. Which one resonates most with you? Where have you allowed a distorted view of wealth, self-worth, or God's promises to limit your life?

2. *Visualize Your Inheritance:* Take a moment to imagine the abundant life God has prepared for you. What does it look like to live unshackled, fully embracing your identity as a child of the King? How would your day-to-day choices, your relationships, or your finances shift if you lived with this mindset?

3. ***Declare Your Identity:*** Out loud, declare who you are in Christ. Speak into existence the promises and truths God has spoken over your life. For example:

- "I am the child of the King of Kings, and His abundance is my inheritance."
- "I am equipped to be a good steward of my resources, and I am breaking free from any mindset that keeps me from living in God's full provision."

ACTION STEPS:

1. ***Prayer Time:*** Set aside 5–10 minutes each day this week to pray about one of the unproductive money mindsets that spoke to you. Ask God to reveal areas where you've unknowingly accepted these mindsets and seek His guidance in breaking free from them.

2. ***Journal Your Journey:*** Write about the financial and spiritual goals you've been hesitant to pursue. What has held you back?

What first step can you take today to begin reclaiming your territory? Keep a record of the mindset shifts and victories God is leading you through.

3. ***Accountability Partner:*** Share one of your financial or spiritual goals with a trusted friend or mentor. Ask them to pray with you and keep you accountable as you begin this journey of breaking free and stepping into your inheritance.

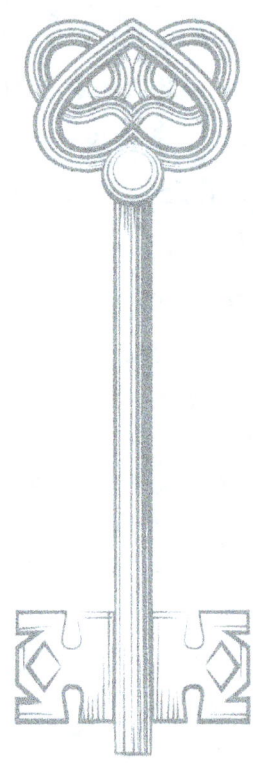

CHAPTER 2:

Destiny, Deliverance, and Drought

DISCOVERING MY DESTINY

During and after the 10-day Daniel Fast, God began to reveal my destiny to me, along with some immediate instructions that I was to complete right away. Looking back, it's clear that these instructions were designed to boost my confidence in my ability to hear God's voice. These were more than tasks—they were a divine calling, a blueprint for my Kingdom assignment.

The first instruction was for me to host a 7-day LIVE IG series, introducing the 7 Unproductive Money Mindsets. It was terrifying at the time! I had never done anything like it before, and being live on Instagram felt like being on stage in front of the world. You can still find that series on my old

THE RIGHTFUL OWNER

Instagram at @towerabovefinance. However, rather than have you search through hundreds of content posts, you can find them here, www.Kiamesheaprewitt.com/resources. I'll warn you—I was super nervous, and my delivery was a bit shaky. But the message? That was straight from God.

That series wasn't just about sharing information; it was about stepping into the role God had assigned me. He was showing me how important this message was—not just for me, but for others who needed to break free from the same strongholds I had dealt with.

A DIVINE TREASURE HUNT

After completing the Instagram series, God didn't stop there. He sent me on what I now see as a spiritual scavenger hunt. I kept hearing the name "Christy Wright" in my spirit, along with the words "Business Boutique." Without much knowledge about her, I felt compelled to search her out online. What I found was her podcast, and after listening, I sensed I wasn't done yet. God was leading me to her conference. Even as I searched for details, doubts filled my mind: the timing was off, I wasn't sure I could afford it, and maybe it had already passed.

34

But here's the thing: God had an answer for every doubt.

When I worried about the money for a ticket? God reminded me of the flight credit I had. When I hesitated about the cost of the conference? My husband encouraged me to invest in a "Premier" ticket. And when I wondered where I would stay, God reminded me that I had lived in Nashville for 10 years—surely someone would open their home to me. And they did.

Every single need I had was met before I even realized I had them. Looking back, I realize that attending this conference wasn't just an event—it was God's setup for the next leap in my faith journey.

THE VIP SHIFT

On the final day of the conference, I signed up for a VIP group session with Christy Wright, which ended up moving me closer to the stage—literally and spiritually. It was my first time sitting in VIP, and though I was physically there, mentally, I kept telling myself I didn't belong. But God was working. Despite the lies of rejection and false humility that played in my head, I stayed in my seat. I wasn't there by accident.

Christy asked for volunteers to share the notes of encouragement we'd written earlier in the conference. I hadn't planned on volunteering, but when my hand shot up, there was no turning back. Standing on that stage, reading aloud what was essentially a note to myself, God began to move through me. The words came out shaky at first, but then something shifted, and I found my voice.

God was using that moment to announce me to the world. It wasn't about popularity or applause—it was about stepping into the authority He had already given me. I remember this moment so vividly: I opened my mouth and the following words burst from within me like the roar of a lioness:

"You are wonderfully & fearfully made. The passion within you was given to you when you were in the depths of the earth. No need to continue to doubt if you are hearing God correctly about that business idea because this is confirmation that you are. This is your time, so rise to the occasion, and be exactly who God has called you to be."

I don't think at that moment, I was able to fully understand the weight of my worth and value, but what I do know
is that my voice released a sound that ushered in a shift in me.

DELIVERANCE BEGINS

You might think this is the part where I share how I received deliverance from the 7 Unproductive Money Mindsets, but the truth is, my journey to full freedom wasn't instantaneous.

After completing the assignments God gave me—hosting the IG series and attending the Business Boutique conference—I should have gone back to Him. I should have asked, "God, did I do this to Your satisfaction? What's next?" Instead, I kept running, assuming I was finished with what He had asked of me.

Had I paused to seek further direction, I'm certain He would have led me through deliverance. Deliverance from the pride that blinded me, the fear that held me back, and the unhealed parts of my heart that still needed God's touch. Without this deliverance, I wasn't operating in full alignment with His plans for me, and that impacted everything.

A SEASON OF DROUGHT

Matthew 13:22 talks about how the deceitfulness of wealth can choke the Word and make it unproductive. That was my life during this time. I had done the work. I had the impact. But my soil wasn't ready. I wasn't fully delivered, and as a result, my efforts felt barren.

The drought wasn't about a lack of action—it was about a lack of fruitfulness. I could see the surface-level progress, but beneath, my heart wasn't fully healed. My business struggled, and even though I had paid off significant debt, there was still a disconnect between me and the abundance God wanted to release into my life.

Without deliverance, without fully addressing the unproductive money mindsets that were still lingering, I was running in circles. I couldn't help others the way I was called to because I hadn't fully received my own freedom. God was preparing me for more, but first, He needed to get me to a place where I could steward the promise well.

Barren land isn't always completely dry—it can produce sparse, stunted growth. That's what my life felt like. I was doing enough to get by, but not enough to thrive. And I realized that being anointed for greatness isn't enough. There are requirements—spiritual, emotional, and practical—that must be met to unlock the fullness of what God has for us.

It's time to **Seize the moment!** This book is about going against what the world says about being successful, which means that we go low so that God can take us higher. Take five minutes or so and ask God if pride is acting as a spiritual blinder in your life.

OWN IT NOW:
Unlock Your Destiny

If you feel like you've been running hard but still coming up empty, it's time to take a deeper look. Have you been acting without seeking God's next steps? Have you allowed old mindsets or strongholds to block your fruitfulness?

This is where deliverance begins—by first acknowledging the places where we need God's healing.

REFLECTION QUESTIONS:

1. In what areas of your life have you taken action without asking God for further guidance?

2. Where do you see unfruitfulness, despite your hard work? What might still need healing for you to fully step into your calling?

ACTION STEPS:

1. *Assess Your Mindsets:* Head to webpage www.kiamesheaprewitt.com to take the *Unproductive Money Mindsets Quiz*. This will help you identify which of the seven mindsets may be holding you back.

2. *Dive Deeper with Free Resources:* My 7-day Instagram series on breaking free from these mindsets is available for free on the website. If you're ready to dig deeper and make lasting change, it's time to engage with these tools. They're designed to help you uncover the strongholds blocking your fruitfulness and guide you through the process of letting them go.

3. *Commit to Deliverance:* It's not enough to recognize the barriers—you have to actively seek God's deliverance. Start by praying for clarity and healing in the areas where you feel barren. Ask God for specific instructions on how to uproot these mindsets and fully embrace your calling.

Remember, this journey isn't just about survival. It's about thriving, stepping into your rightful place as a child of the King, and living in the fullness of what God has planned for you.

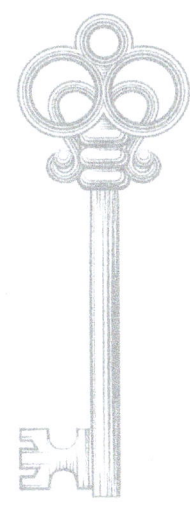

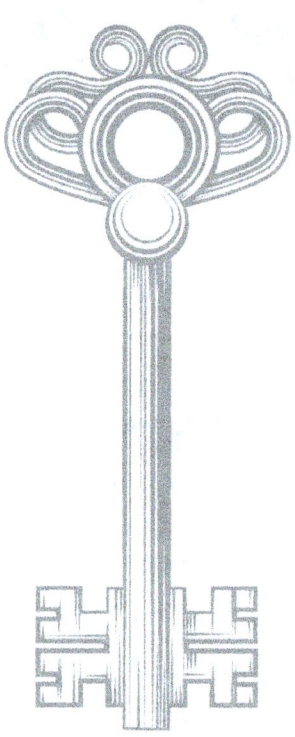

CHAPTER 3

Financial Fraudulence Syndrome (FFS)

What would you do if you woke up tomorrow in your dream house? Yes, the dream kitchen and the spa-like bathroom you've always wanted. You check your bank account, and the financial promises God made to you years ago have come to pass. I'm curious—how would you react? Would feelings of unworthiness hit you like a ton of bricks as you wait for someone to knock on your door and say it was all a mistake? Would you call the bank, asking them to trace the seven-figure deposit? Maybe you'd scramble to "even the scales" by giving away handbags or donating a large sum of money, trying to balance out the size of the blessing?

After years of working with one-on-one coaching clients, I've noticed a pattern: many women feel they lack the competency to manage and discuss financial matters. Even when they receive an increase, they feel unworthy, fearing they'll misuse the blessing, despite having a solid financial plan. For women of color with Christian backgrounds, I've observed an additional layer—the way we perceive how Jesus views wealth can deeply affect our relationship with it.

It makes sense, right? Whether or not we are active in our faith today, many of us still carry the beliefs we were raised with. But here's the problem: if you were taught to view wealth as evil or feared that being wealthy would make you unfit for heaven, you may have developed a complicated, even conflicted, relationship with money. And yet, deep down, since you were a little girl, God gave you visions, dreams, and affirmations that you were called to wealth. But growing up in an environment that conditioned you to think wealthy people were corrupt makes that promise hard to accept.

THE CONTRADICTIONS OF FFS

At the crossroads of this internal conflict is something I call *Financial Fraudulence Syndrome* (FFS). FFS is the entanglement of worthiness contradictions that affect how you perceive and manage wealth. It leads to self-sabotage, mismanagement of the wealth you currently have, and an inability to embrace future abundance. It's a battle between how you see yourself, how you perceive God views wealth, and how worthy you believe you are of success.

FFS doesn't discriminate. It affects highly successful women, those always striving for new heights, and especially women of color, given our history of being placed at the bottom of the social and economic ladder. FFS shows up in various ways, often through the lens of the 7 Unproductive Money Mindsets and Behaviors that I introduced earlier.

WEARING A PERSONA

When I reflect on the early days of my Kingdom-building journey, I now see how I created a persona to shield myself from feelings of inadequacy. I didn't feel worthy of God's promises, so I adopted an identity of how I *thought* successful people should look and act. In doing so, I was, in effect, telling God, "You didn't make the right choice." This false identity may have gotten me through sales calls and client interactions, but it came from a place of spiritual blindness—driven by pride.

I was following the "fake it till you make it" philosophy, projecting a false sense of ownership over my Kingdom assignment. But in my heart, I wasn't convinced that God had chosen the right person for the job. You cannot cover up depression, fear, and feelings of unworthiness by playing dress-up. No amount of affirmations or positive thinking can unlock your Kingdom inheritance if true spiritual pruning hasn't taken place. Hiding behind a persona only delays deliverance and leads to destruction.

You know you're doing a great job faking it when people don't even ask if you need help—they assume you have it all together. This creates a dangerous cycle. On one hand, your spiritual blindness convinces you that things aren't as bad as they seem, leaving no room for self-accountability. On the other hand, by misleading those around you, you miss out on external accountability.

MY TURNING POINT

Eventually, God let me wear myself out. After two years of striving in my own strength, I found myself drained—financially, spiritually, and emotionally. But in His mercy, God didn't give up on me. Instead, He set the stage to expose my true intentions.

It all began when I hosted an online challenge to promote a new coaching program. I threw everything into this event, sure that it would be my big breakthrough. The challenge had impressive registration numbers, but it didn't translate into financial success. Despite how "successful" it appeared on the outside, I felt empty inside. The event had become a playground for the spirit of mammon, and I didn't even realize it.

You see, I had fallen into the trap of thinking money could bring me what only God can give: security, significance, identity, power, and freedom. I was so tired of struggling that I believed mammon's empty promises. I didn't realize I was worshiping the very thing God was trying to free me from.

AN INVITATION FOR DELIVERANCE

After the challenge, I felt humiliated and confused. Where had I gone wrong? I had followed God's instructions—or so I thought. I felt like a fraud, angry with God for leading me down a path that didn't bring the breakthrough I expected. I began to entertain thoughts of abandoning my Kingdom assignment altogether.

But God wasn't finished with me. Night after night, I felt the nudge to wake up and spend time with Him. I struggled, physically weighed down by what felt like a spiritual attack. Eventually, I realized I had allowed room for demonic forces to take hold in my life. By not fully relying on God, I had left the door open for the enemy to operate freely.

God never gave up on me, though. He could have easily given someone else my Kingdom assignment, but He saw me as the rightful owner. Slowly, He led me through a process of surrender—of taking off the masks I had worn and admitting my deep need for His help.

OVERCOMING FFS

One month later, I hosted my first Kingdom Financial Healing Retreat, a space for leaders to rest and heal in the area of their finances. I was guiding others through deliverance, but God wasn't about to let me leave without experiencing it myself. After a stubborn demonic attack, I finally received my own deliverance.

What I didn't realize until much later was that I had come into agreement with the spirit of mammon long before. The spirit of mammon, which brings poverty, lack, fear, and pride, had been controlling parts of my life. Breaking free wasn't just a matter of willpower; it required spiritual deliverance and intentionally renewing my mind with the Word of God.

That's why I created my **Primed for Prosperity Wealth Affirmation Cards**—because the fight against these demonic spirits requires strategy. They don't fight fair, and we need to be spiritually prepared to break free from their grip. If you're in a season of financial healing, it's crucial to change your language around money, distance yourself from people who align with mammon, and consistently renew your mind with God's truth.

Seize the Moment

If you are interested in starting your journey to financial healing, then be sure to head to our Patreon community to grab your *5 complimentary affirmation cards*.

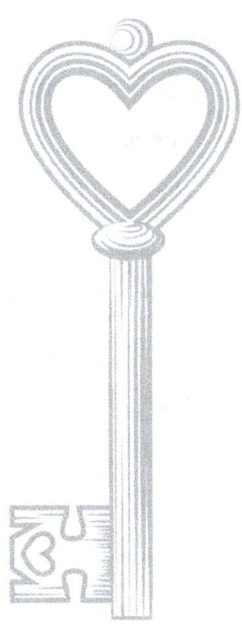

OWN IT NOW:
Break Free from FFS

FFS can creep in subtly, impacting how you perceive, manage, and grow wealth. But awareness is the first step in overcoming it. Here's how you can start to break free:

REFLECTION QUESTIONS:

1. Do you feel like you've been wearing a "persona" to hide feelings of unworthiness when it comes to wealth or success?

2. Where in your life have you agreed with the spirit of mammon, even unknowingly? What are the areas where you feel controlled by fear, lack, or pride?

ACTION STEPS:

1. *Start Your Journey to Financial Healing:* If you still haven't taken the *Unproductive Money Mindsets Quiz*, be sure to do so today. This will help you assess which mindsets may be holding you back from fully walking in God's financial promises for your life.

2. *Activate the Power of Words:* As you start to break free from FFS, use the *Primed for Prosperity Wealth Affirmation Cards* to replace the lies of lack with God's truth about abundance. These cards are specifically designed to help you change your language around money and declare what God says about your financial future.

3. *Go Deeper:* If you're ready for a deeper dive into financial healing and deliverance, explore the free 7-day Instagram series I created to walk you through this process and go back to the welcome video and listen to the prayer I spoke over you as you begin this journey.

Remember, freedom comes through deliverance and transformation. This isn't about managing your finances better—it's about breaking free from the lies that have kept you from fully stepping into your financial inheritance.

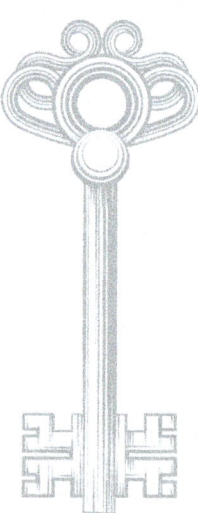

CHAPTER 4:

Healed, Empty, &
Things Got Worse

In the previous chapter, we explored how *Financial Fraud-ulence Syndrome (FFS)* is tied to demonic spirits and manifests through the 7 Unproductive Money Mindsets. From my experience, the only way to sever these mindsets at the root is through spiritual deliverance. You can do all the things—attend conferences, follow strategies, and implement best practices—but only the work Jesus did on the cross can break the unproductive cycles we face around wealth.

Poverty is a direct manifestation of the enemy's agenda, as outlined in John 10:10: "to kill, steal, and destroy." This spirit will fight hard to remain attached to your life. Deliverance isn't just a moment; it's often a process that unfolds over time.

THE BATTLE AFTER DELIVERANCE

The night of my financial healing retreat marked the beginning of my deliverance journey, but I didn't know it was just the start. A couple of weeks later, I woke up in the middle of the night with intense "heartburn." This wasn't your typical discomfort; I felt an overwhelming urge to go to my prayer closet and worship God. But, as you can imagine, the weight of sleep laid heavily on me, and getting out of bed felt like an impossible task.

Eventually, I dragged myself to the prayer closet. I couldn't find the words at first, but a song came to me, and I began to sing it softly. The heartburn would leave for a moment, then return, like an unseen force pushing back against my worship. Finally, I saw an angel standing before me, and as it appeared, I felt a sense of peace, like the pain was gone for good. I knew some deliverance had taken place that night, but I wasn't fully healed yet.

EMPTYING: PRUNING AND REFINING

One morning a couple of weeks later, I woke up feeling terrible. I had a scheduled "Prayer for Your Finances" session and thought there was no way I'd be able to lead it. After much prayer and a sense of obligation to follow through, I managed to host it but immediately went to lie down afterward.

Now, I'm not trying to gross you out, but what happened next was intense. I couldn't keep anything down—not food, not water. It seemed like my body was rejecting everything, and I initially thought it was a demonic attack. After 1.5 days bedridden, I realized that God was allowing this to happen. I couldn't make sense of it in the moment, but looking back, I now see that God was purging me. Physically, I was weak, but spiritually, He was preparing me for the breakthrough that was coming.

This experience was uncomfortable, painful, and inconvenient, not just for me but for my family. I was in bed for nearly three days, experiencing waves of nausea that wouldn't let up. It felt like a prophetic message—that this purging process was making way for something bigger. I couldn't understand why it was happening, but I had to trust that God had a reason.

WHY THE PURGING PROCESS?

I believe there were three reasons for this accelerated purging:

1. **Completion of Deliverance**: During the retreat, I had heard that the spirit I was battling was stubborn. This purging process was necessary to fully rid me of the spirit of mammon and its stronghold over my life.

2. **Removing Traces and Residue**: God was cleansing me, removing any markers that had allowed these spirits entry into my life. He was washing away any residue that could pull me back into bondage. I needed to be fully prepared for what He had in store.

3. **Preparation for a New Birth**: God was ready to birth something new through me—a new nation, a new territory, a new assignment. But in order to step into it, I had to be completely free.

THE STRUGGLE AFTER DELIVERANCE

Here's the part no one really tells you: things didn't get better immediately after deliverance. In fact, in some ways, they got worse. God continued to prune my life in uncomfortable ways. He took away clients, spiritual and professional coverings, and other support systems. I felt like everything I had left was being stripped away.

I was spiritually fragile, confused, and desperate for answers. "God, what are you doing?" I cried out. The attacks weren't just hitting my business—they were hitting our household finances too. It felt unfair. My husband and I were tithers, we made budgets, we were faithful Kingdom citizens, so why were we going through this?

Even when we tried to sell our investment property, we encountered two scams that took even our realtor by surprise. It felt like we were surrounded by monitoring spirits, watching and waiting for us to slip up. I was convinced I was on the brink of a nervous breakdown.

THE REALITY OF DELIVERANCE

What I learned through this season is that deliverance is not a one-time event. It happens over time, often slowly. You're likely not the first person in your bloodline to experience FFS, and cutting it off at the root requires a determined mindset.

Therapy is great, but therapy alone cannot destroy FFS. It's tied to generational strongholds, and the spirit of mammon and its cousins—poverty and lack—will fight to keep you stuck. They don't want you to succeed. They know that if you do, you'll become a fruitful Kingdom citizen, bearing the fruit God intended for you all along.

If you're going through your own deliverance process, understand that it may take time before you see the fruit of your breakthrough. But trust that God is refining you, just like He refined me. The feeling of being forsaken? God used it to refine my husband and me for the blessings that were on the way.

Seize the Moment

Deliverance is a process. It's not a quick fix but a journey of pruning and refinement. Take a moment to reflect on areas where you may be holding onto residue of the spirits of mammon, poverty, or lack. Ask God to reveal what still needs to be purged from your life and invite Him to continue the work He started.

OWN IT NOW:
Embrace the Refining Process

In seasons of deliverance, it's easy to feel discouraged when things seem to get worse before they get better. But remember, God is refining you for a purpose. Here's how you can begin to embrace the process and prepare for the blessings to come:

REFLECTION QUESTIONS:

1. Where in your life do you feel like you're still holding onto residue from spirits like mammon, poverty, or lack?

2. What areas of your life need further pruning for you to step into the fullness of what God has prepared for you?

ACTION STEPS:

1. *Seek Further Deliverance:* If you're in a similar place and still struggling with unproductive money mindsets, take the next step

by visiting [Kiameshea Prewitt | Kingdom Financial Wellness - YouTube](#). There, you can take the *Unproductive Money Mindsets Quiz* and identify the strongholds that may still have a grip on you.

2. ***Stay Spiritually Sharp:*** If you're navigating the refining process, don't do it alone. Explore the resources available on my Patreon, including free tools like the *Primed for Prosperity Wealth Affirmation Cards* to help you stay aligned with God's promises during this season of pruning.

3. **Pray with Intention**: God often brings deliverance through persistent prayer. If you're ready to go deeper, I encourage you to join the *Prayer for Your Finances with KP* sessions on my youtube channel. These guided prayer sessions are designed to equip you with the spiritual tools needed for breakthrough.

Remember, God's timing is perfect. Even when things feel like they're falling apart, He is strategically preparing you for the blessings that are on the way. Stay in the process, and trust that He is purging what no longer serves you to make room for His abundance

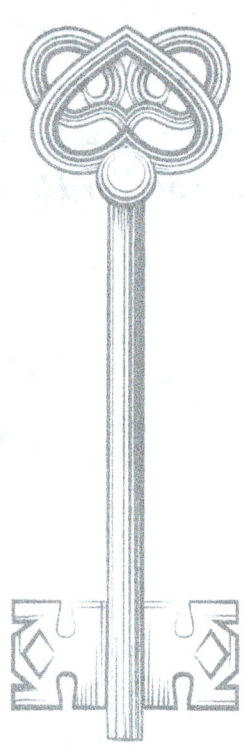

CHAPTER 5

Acceptance & Agreement

Amidst all the chaos swirling in my life, I finally decided to start therapy. I was struggling deeply with unworthiness, and even though I had taken major steps in my professional journey—like joining a prestigious coaching program—I felt like a fraud. This wasn't just any coaching program. The women in this room were making 6, 7, and even 8 figures, and they exuded a level of ambition, experience, and fearlessness that made me feel small. Being among them only amplified my insecurities.

So here I was, having paid five figures to be part of this incredible coaching program, yet it took me *four weeks* just to muster up the courage to engage. I couldn't understand what was wrong with me. Why wasn't I showing up like I had in the past? What was holding me back? Determined to figure it out, I started therapy.

CAME OUT OF AGREEMENT WITH THE ENEMY'S PLAN

The therapist I found was filled with the Holy Spirit, and after two months of working together, she gave me life-changing advice: fast once a week and focus on coming out of agreement with three specific spirits—rejection, people-pleasing, and the orphan spirit. She also instructed me to come into agreement with the spirit of adoption and the fire of the Holy Spirit. I submitted to her instructions, and as soon as I did, I began to see God shift things in my life.

The pain and suffering didn't immediately disappear, but this process taught me something critical: the first step to ownership is agreement with God. And agreement with God requires obedience. Our choices are simple—we either agree with God or with Satan. There's no in-between.

As Matthew 17:20-21 says, "Because of your little faith... if you have faith the size of a mustard seed, you will tell this mountain, 'Move from here to there,' and it will move. Nothing will be impossible for you. However, this kind does not come out except by prayer and fasting."

My therapist explained that by allowing fear of rejection, people-pleasing, and the orphan spirit to dominate my life,

I was unwillingly coming into agreement with the enemy's plan. Each time I shrank back, entertained doubt, or walked in double-mindedness, I was aligning myself with Satan's mission of destruction. We already know what his plans are—he comes to steal, kill, and destroy.

But it wasn't enough to just pray these spirits away. My therapist understood that I had to *war* against them. Each week, as I fasted and prayed, I focused on one of these spirits. I reminded myself who I was and, more importantly, who I belonged to—God. Through prayer and fasting, I began to uncover the origins of these spirits. Rejection, for instance, had attached itself to me when my birth father left when I was only two years old. It was strengthened by bullying at school and compounded by a lifetime of feeling misunderstood. Over the years, rejection became part of my identity, so much so that I often rejected others before they had a chance to reject me.

But here's the hard part: coming into agreement with God's spirit of *acceptance* requires vulnerability. It demands faith. And faith means letting go of control.

As Hebrews 11:6 says, "Now without faith, it is impossible to please God, for the one who draws near to Him must believe that He exists and rewards those who seek Him."

It was humbling to realize how often I had rejected God's plans for me. No wonder I hadn't unlocked the fullness of what He had promised for me and my bloodline! As I began to reject the spirit of rejection, I also started seeing myself as a true daughter of the Most High God. In the process, I deconstructed my fears around people-pleasing. I had been looking to people for my worth instead of to God. When I placed God back in His rightful position, it helped me appreciate favor with man, but in a healthy, balanced way.

Perhaps the reason you haven't unlocked everything God has in store for you is that, like me, you've rejected His plans—or maybe you've made people an idol.

COMING INTO AGREEMENT WITH GOD

Around the same time I was going through therapy, my husband and I began the process of purchasing a lot to build a house in the DFW area. We were still in North Carolina, so the builder's assistant would send us periodic updates. One day, she sent a photo of the lot with a big sign that had the word "PENDING" written across it.

When I shared this with my therapist, she told me that she believed I was also in a "pending" state. She said God kept giving her the same vision week after week—that I was *at a standstill*. Ironically, our house-building process had also stalled. I grew frustrated. "How could I be at a stand-still?" I wondered. I was doing everything I was supposed to—everything God had asked of me.

So, what was I missing? How could I take ownership of who God says I am and the territory He said belonged to me?

THE POWER OF AGREEMENT

When Mary was told she would conceive and give birth to the Son of God, she came into agreement with her Kingdom assignment through her words:

"I am the Lord's servant," Mary answered. "May your word to me be fulfilled." - Luke 1:38

Similarly, when Jehu was anointed as the 10th King of Israel, it took hearing his own words to trigger an activation. He came into agreement with his Kingdom assignment:

"...So Jehu said, 'He told me, 'This is what the Lord says: I anoint you king over Israel.' Each man quickly took his garment and put it under Jehu on the bare steps. They blew the trumpet and shouted, 'Jehu is king!'" - 2 Kings 9:12-13

There is undeniable power in our words. They change our thoughts, which then changes our behavior. God doesn't need us to come into agreement for *His* sake—He's already in control. He requires us to speak His promises for *our* sake, so that we can align ourselves with His plans.

Coming into agreement with God means submitting our will, our plans, and even our dreams to Him. Part of the reason we haven't unlocked our promises is that we've been trying to control *how* God blesses us. But God is not a genie. He's our Lord and King. Submitting means we have to lay our vision boards, financial goals, and 5-year plans at His feet and trust His process.

URGENCY TO PRAY

As you submit to the process, prepare for a new normal. Get ready for the standard to rise. This goes for how God wants to bless you, but also for what will be required of you to steward your destiny.

My new normal required me to go lower—lower in prayer, lower in praise, lower in persistence. Life wasn't easy. In fact, it was the hardest it had ever been. It felt like every time we had hope, it was snatched away. Even after years of disappointment and spiritual attacks, I felt an urgency to pray more often. At first, I resisted. But eventually, I submitted to the urge.

In my time with God, it was like I was learning to pray all over again. Some days I didn't know what to say. Other days, I had no words at all. But through this process, God taught me *how* to pray, and more importantly, *why* prayer would be critical for the places He was taking me.

Have you felt the nudge to spend more time with God? That's Him calling you to receive strategy and preparation for your Kingdom assignment.

Seize the Moment

God is calling you into agreement with Him. If you've been feeling a nudge to pray or spend more time in His presence, don't ignore it. This is the time for preparation. This is the time to position yourself to receive the blessings He has in store.

OWN IT NOW:
Position Yourself for Agreement

Now that you understand the power of coming into agreement with God's plans, it's time to take action. Here are some steps to help you stay aligned and focused on His promises for your life:

REFLECTION QUESTIONS:

1. Are there areas where you have unknowingly rejected God's plans or tried to control how He blesses you?

2. How can you intentionally come into agreement with God's promises through your words, prayers, and daily actions?

ACTION STEPS:

1. *Fast and Pray:* If you're struggling to come into agreement with God's plans, consider a weekly fast, focusing on any spirits or strongholds that need to be broken. For additional

guidance on this, head over to webpage www.kiamesheaprewitt.com and download the free *Breakthrough Fasting Guide*.

2. **Speak Life**: There is power in your words. Start affirming God's promises over your life with the *Primed for Prosperity Wealth Affirmations*. Elevate your affirmations and speak them over your life up to 3x daily.

3. ***Pray for Strategy:*** God wants to give you strategic insight for your Kingdom assignment. If you're ready to go deeper, I have crafted the Unproductive Money Mindsets Prayer just for you. It's designed to equip you with the tools needed to break free from spiritual strongholds.

Remember, as you come into agreement with God, He will open doors you never imagined possible. But first, it requires submission, obedience, and intentional prayer

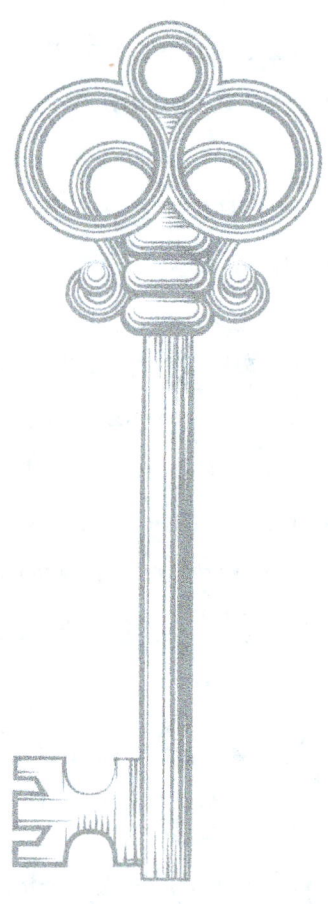

CHAPTER 6:

Seize & Occupy

We've established that the first step to taking ownership of our Kingdom territory is coming into agreement with God's plans through the power of our words. But what comes next? After agreement, we must *seize* and *occupy*.

When we hear the terms "seize and occupy," we often think of natural tasks, especially in the context of war. However, God required me to seize and occupy in the *spirit* so that I could manifest those victories in the *natural*—as is evident in this book I'm writing now. Ephesians 6:12 reminds us, "For we wrestle not against flesh and blood, but against principalities, against powers, against the rulers of the darkness of this world, against spiritual wickedness in high places."

To seize and occupy, God led me into the courts of heaven to claim what rightfully belonged to me. Months before this,

He had prepared me by having me read Robert Henderson's book, *Operating in the Courts of Heaven*. I learned that the enemy is our accuser, and he builds cases against us, using not only our sins but also the sins of our husbands, mothers, fathers, and even grandparents. Just like in an earthly courtroom, if we don't show up to defend our case, we risk forfeiture. So, I went through the process God had shown me and stood before Him in the courts of heaven to seize back what the enemy had unlawfully taken—not just from me, but from my bloodline. God also instructed me to take my husband into the courts with me, and we went together.

SPIRITUAL WARFARE IN THE COURTS OF HEAVEN

If you had asked me about going into a heavenly realm months before this moment, I would have felt nervous and uneasy. But by then, the intimacy I had cultivated with God gave me confidence that He had my back. My focus wasn't on the "how" of it all, but on reclaiming what was owed to me. At first, I wasn't sure I was doing it right, but soon I sensed an angelic presence around me. It was a powerful experience.

After going into the courts of heaven, my confidence in my Kingdom identity and assignment soared. I noticed a shift in my motivation around executing my Kingdom assignment. Something clicked inside me—I no longer saw this journey as simply about *me* or my abilities, but about God. I felt like an officer in the Kingdom of Heaven with a duty to fulfill, bigger than myself. Financial Fraudulence Syndrome (FFS) causes us to be self-centered, but God requires us to be *God-centered* in order to fulfill all He has planned for us.

This experience was the "seize" part of my journey. But now, it was time to *occupy*.

SEIZING VS. OCCUPYING

Seizing is a critical step that cannot be skipped. That's why this book is called *The Rightful Owner* and not just "Occupy" or "The Owner." Someone or something is currently occupying territory that is *not legally theirs* because it belongs to you. Your job is to take it back, starting with the spiritual realm.

Once I had seized the territory, occupying it required a few things. First, I had to stay connected to my intel source—God—so He could give me the lay of the land. He became my tour guide, showing me how to navigate this unfamiliar space. This required me to continually study His Word and be intentional about my prayer strategy.

I had to set aside specific times to seek God as a daughter and other times to approach Him as an ambassador of the

Kingdom of Heaven. This balance was crucial, reminding me that I am first and foremost His daughter. Maintaining intimacy with God is a superpower against the enemy. This intimacy reaffirms my Kingdom identity and spiritually satisfies me, making the enemy's temptations less appealing because my spirit is more nourished than my flesh. While I'm not perfect at this balance, I find that most times, I can get victory over the enemy's schemes.

STRETCHING BEYOND COMFORT ZONES

Occupying territory also meant stepping out of my comfort zone and tackling the challenging tasks I had avoided in the past. These represented areas of my inheritance that belonged to me, but I had avoided them because they didn't come easily. Now, it was time to walk confidently into uncharted territory.

For me, this meant writing my first book (which you're reading right now) and redefining Tower Above's services to be a corporate financial wellness solution. God also wanted me to take my rightful place as a thought leader. The thought of being a thought leader overwhelmed me with fear. I imagined being interviewed on TV, stumped by tough questions or challenged in my beliefs, unable to defend myself.

But despite these fears, I gave God my "Yes," and He handled the rest. I followed His leading, and every time there was an open door waiting for me. There were even moments when the door seemed closed, but I would go back to God, explain the situation, and He would quickly reveal the next steps to open it. As a result, I experienced growth at a healthy, sustainable pace.

Faith was essential in this process. Whenever I felt my faith waning, I asked God to help my unbelief, and He always did.

OPERATING IN WISDOM

The final but crucial step in occupying new territory is operating in wisdom. During this season, God had me practice what I would need to perfect in the years to come—self-control and discernment about what to share and with whom. As the queen of my territory, I learned that I cannot share my nation's sensitive intel with just anyone. This was hard for me because I wanted to tell everyone about the exciting things God was doing in my life. But He constantly reminded me that this information was on a need-to-know basis.

God had me moving behind closed doors to maintain and protect my new territory. Not everyone needed to know, and that was okay.

Seize the Moment

God is ready to bless you beyond what you've imagined, but first, you need to seize what is rightfully yours in the spiritual realm and then occupy your newfound territory in the natural. Ask Him today: What territory are You calling me to seize? Where do You need me to step up in faith and occupy? Don't skip the seize step—it's a key part of the journey.

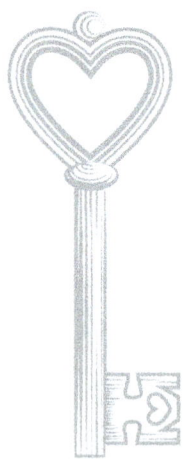

OWN IT NOW:
Seize Your Spiritual Territory

Now that you understand the importance of both seizing and occupying, it's time to take action. Here are some steps to help you move forward:

REFLECTION QUESTIONS:

1. What territory (spiritual or natural) do you sense the enemy is unlawfully occupying in your life?

2. Have you been avoiding any uncomfortable or challenging tasks that represent unclaimed territory?

Taking Action on Your Next Steps

Now that you know it's time to seize and occupy, what's your next move? Here are some action steps to help you move forward thoughtfully:

1. ***Evaluate Your Territory:*** Take a moment to reflect on areas of your life where the enemy may be unlawfully occupying your territory. Is it your finances? Your relationships? Your purpose? Identify where God is calling you to reclaim what is rightfully yours.

2. ***Strengthen Your Intimacy with God:*** Make space for intentional time with God. Set aside moments to simply rest in His presence as His daughter, and also create time to seek His direction as His ambassador. Listen carefully to His strategy for your life.

3. ***Step Out of Your Comfort Zone:*** Identify one thing God is calling you to do that feels challenging or overwhelming. It might be a new project, a conversation, or expanding into a new area of life. Commit to taking that first step in faith.

4. ***Ask for Wisdom:*** Before making major decisions or sharing sensitive information, ask God for wisdom. Take time to discern what to

share and with whom. Not every opportunity is meant to be public, and wisdom will help you protect the territory you're occupying.

5. **Celebrate Small Wins**: As you step out and begin to occupy your new territory, don't forget to celebrate each small victory along the way. Acknowledge God's faithfulness and give yourself credit for walking in faith!

Remember, this is a process of growth and refinement. You're not meant to do it perfectly. Just keep moving forward, trusting that God is leading you, step by step, into your Kingdom inheritance.

As you step forward in faith and obedience, remember that God is with you, guiding you every step of the way. Seize what is yours, occupy it, and walk confidently into your Kingdom inheritance.

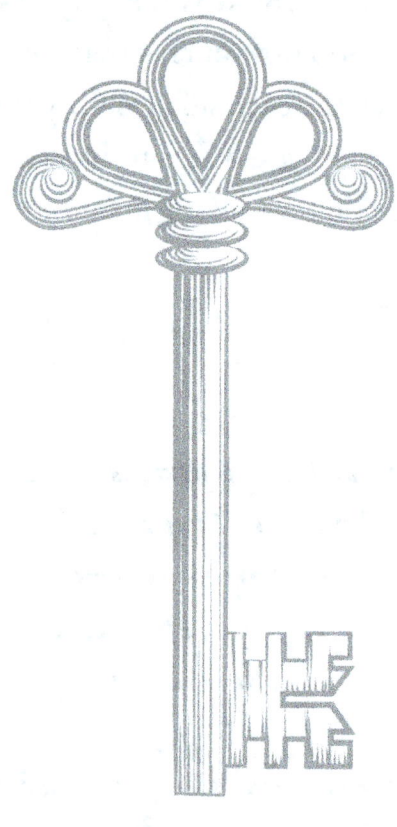

CHAPTER 7:

Reclaim with Urgency

One key thing about tactical mission terms like "seize" and "occupy" is that these actions are taken in the middle of a war—and they happen swiftly. They are precise, strategic tasks that require quick execution. In this spiritual war, there's no time for double-mindedness or for any of the symptoms of Financial Fraudulence Syndrome (FFS) to creep in. We have to keep our attention locked on our intel source—God—and move with purpose.

I've heard countless stories of people waiting on the Lord. You know the phrase: "I'm still waiting on the Lord." To be honest, I used to be one of those people. I would wait and wait. And yes, there is a season of waiting that is a necessary part of the walk with God. But recently, I've become convinced that, often, when God is calling you to move, He's actually *waiting on you.*

But here's the thing: while you want to move swiftly, you also need to move with God. I've learned that there is an art to moving fast while staying in alignment with Him. My desire is to walk in step with God. I might not always know where I'm going, and I'm fully dependent on Him to lead, but I've learned to focus on what He's given me to do in the moment. I walk through each step *with* Him, talking to Him along the way, asking for guidance, and making sure I don't take off ahead of Him.

There have been times when God, in His grace, will give me a glimpse of two or three steps ahead to provide some context. But even when I can see a little further ahead, I hold His hand through each step. I want to stay right beside Him.

It's not just about not wanting to leave God's presence—it's also about strategic timing. There is power in God's appointed timing. There's a window of grace that is given when we *reclaim with urgency*.

DON'T BE SLOTHFUL

"Laziness induces deep sleep, and a lazy person will go hungry." —Proverbs 19:15

Slothfulness isn't just about laziness or apathy—it also includes avoidance and procrastination. And where there is avoidance, there is disobedience. Some people might call it "delayed obedience" to soften the blow, but disobedience is still disobedience. If we're being disobedient, we're coming out of agreement with God's plans for us—and that's exactly what the enemy wants.

If you're someone who tends to avoid what needs to be done, it's helpful to have people in your life who can hold you accountable. It's even better if you allow them to call you out when necessary. The Holy Spirit is also great at nudging you when you're avoiding something—so ask for His help, too. Be self-aware and know what triggers your avoidance.

Laziness can also show up in our execution. I'm learning the importance of "progress over perfection," but that doesn't mean we should throw things together haphazardly. I know you're a high-achieving woman, and this probably isn't something you struggle with often, but it's worth mentioning. As representatives of the Kingdom, a certain standard of excellence is expected of us from God.

When God gives me an assignment now, I ask for the capacity to think through His instructions thoroughly. I ask questions. I don't rush to complete projects like I might have done in the past. God has taught me this valuable concept of "Slowing down, so that He can Speed Me Up." Essentially, when I take the time to do things right the first time, God can then accelerate my work.

Remember, you have a new normal now. Don't expect to go back to your life and move forward as if nothing has changed.

Seize the Moment

In this chapter, we've seen how vital it is to move quickly but in alignment with God. There is urgency in the reclaiming of your spiritual inheritance, and the time is now. Are there areas in your life where God has been prompting you to take action, but you've been hesitant? Perhaps fear, avoidance, or even laziness has kept you from fully reclaiming what is rightfully yours.

This is your call to action: Seize and occupy the territory God has given you. Don't wait. Don't hesitate. Step into your calling, and trust that as you move with God, He will lead you every step of the way.

OWN IT NOW:
Practical Steps to Reclaim with Urgency

1. *Identify What's Blocking You:* Take a moment to reflect. Is there an area in your life where you've been avoiding action? Whether it's fear, doubt, or procrastination, identify the root of the hesitation so you can address it.

2. *Check In With God:* Are you in step with God, or are you running ahead of Him? Spend time in prayer and ask God to show you where you may have jumped ahead or fallen behind. Commit to walking in sync with His timing.

3. *Find Accountability:* Surround yourself with people who will lovingly hold you accountable. Whether it's a trusted friend, mentor, or prayer partner, make sure you have someone who can help you stay focused and aligned with God's plans.

4. ***Execute with Excellence:*** As you step out to reclaim what is yours, don't cut corners. God has given you this territory, and He's called you to steward it well. Take time to execute with excellence, knowing that it honors Him.

5. ***Celebrate Progress***: Even as you move with urgency, celebrate the small wins along the way. Each step of faith, each act of obedience, brings you closer to fully occupying your territory.

You are in a spiritual battle, but God has equipped you with everything you need to win. Now is the time to seize what is yours and occupy your rightful place. Step out in faith, trust God's timing, and move with urgency.

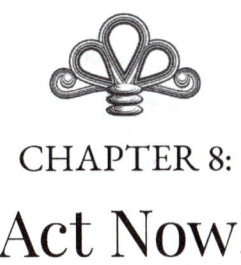

CHAPTER 8

Act Now!

As you move forward, reclaiming your ownership with urgency, there are some warnings I wish someone had given me. The enemy is not all-knowing, but because he once fell from heaven, he understands how the heavenly realm operates. So, when he sees legions of angels dispatched on your behalf, he will be furious. He'll know he's been defeated in keeping you from taking your rightful position, and he will throw everything in his arsenal at you as a last resort to stop you from moving forward. I remember, at this very point, when the enemy attacked me through dreams, thoughts, and even caused havoc in my household. My time with God became crucial, providing a lifeline that helped me navigate these trials.

FFS MAY TRY TO CREEP BACK IN

Financial Fraudulence Syndrome (FFS) isn't something you wake up with one day. It develops over time, and you might have unconsciously built your identity around it. FFS could even be your coping mechanism when you're on the brink of success. So, as you step into your new season and feel the symptoms of FFS trying to reappear, understand that this is a *threshold moment*. It's the final battle between the old and the new. Will you cross over into the fullness of God's promises, or will you allow the past to pull you back?

KINGDOM AUTHORITY IS YOURS— CHOOSE WISELY

You are at a crossroads, woman of God. Right now, you have a critical choice to make. What will you choose? The door of opportunity God has placed before you is wide open. It's everything you've been praying for, but the spirit of doubt may try to sneak in, taunting you: *Are you enough? Can you really sustain the new normal that's ahead?*

What you might not realize is that your fear of failure is really a *fear of success*. Yes, it sounds strange because you've accomplished so much already. But what lies ahead is different—it's beyond your strength. The heights of success God is taking you to will feel so overwhelming, you'll know without a doubt that it's Him opening those doors. These are places where you will feel out of your depth, yet destined to be.

On the other hand, there's always the familiar. You could fall back into old patterns of self-sabotage and allow FFS to keep its grip on your life. You wouldn't be the first person to do this—many have chosen comfort over calling, convincing themselves it doesn't take "all that" to please God. But deep down, you know the truth.

The choice is yours.

YOU MAY FEEL CONFINED

Your "yes" to God is costly. What was once normal can't go with you to your new territory. God may ask you to cut off certain things—like what you watch, what you consume, or even some relationships. For me, I had to limit TV to channels like HGTV and Food Network. My diet started to change too, as God was even altering my tastes, making certain foods less appealing. I lost friendships that were dear to me during this season, which was hard, especially since I had just found friends who truly understood me. Yet, when I fully committed to my "yes," God swiftly sent new, godly friendships into my life.

All of these changes—happening at once—made me feel out of control. I even had a dream where I was in prison, symbolizing how trapped I felt. But looking back, I see that God was being strategic. Everything He told me to let go of was for my protection and to help me keep Him as the priority in my life. The enemy loves to attack us through what we consume—what we see, hear, and speak. Those are gateways to our hearts. God knew exactly what I would need to sustain and maintain my new normal, so He was helping me cut away what could hinder my success.

Living like a queen requires a higher standard. At first, this felt overwhelming—so much needed to change. The enemy used this to make me feel like life would be boring and joyless in my new season. But God showed me that I wasn't resisting the change out of disobedience; I was just nervous. I urge you, too, to see this pruning process not as a burden but as your Esther moment of preparation.

ACTIVATE THE ANOINTING: A SPIRITUAL BREAKTHROUGH

In a quiet place behind closed doors, God anointed me. I felt oil in the spirit dripping down from my head, signifying that I had stepped into a new realm of authority and purpose. It was a moment I knew I had been prepared for—a shift so profound, I could sense it in every part of my being. This was no ordinary experience; it was the activation of the anointing that had been lying dormant within me. God had shown me through His Word and teachings that the anointing needed to be *activated* by declaring and standing in agreement with His promises over my life.

Immediately after this moment, I was placed in situations that demanded I step fully into my authority. There was no room for hesitation. Deliverance took place, and in the spirit, I saw a crown placed upon my head—a sign that I had been commissioned, not just for the battle I was in, but for the battles yet to come. I had to learn how to walk in this newfound power, and how to use it effectively to reclaim what was rightfully mine.

The anointing is not something we wait to feel—it's something we *activate* through prayer, fasting, and strategic spiritual alignment. Here, I want to share with you my 3 step ACT Now formula and *Financial Deliverance Prayer* system that will help you activate the anointing over your finances and guide you in reclaiming the abundance God has prepared for you.

A.C.T. NOW: YOUR 3-STEP FORMULA FOR RIGHTFUL OWNERSHIP

STEP 1:
ACCEPT & AGREE

The first step to financial deliverance is acceptance. You need to fully accept where you are and come into agreement with God's vision for your finances. This involves acknowledging the lies you may have believed about your worth, money, and success. It's time to uproot those lies and replace them with God's truth.

Prayer of Acceptance: "Father God, I accept where I am today—no matter how far from financial abundance it may seem. I come into full agreement with Your plans for my life. I release every lie the enemy has spoken over me, and I replace it with the truth that I am worthy of wealth, favor, and prosperity. I align myself with Your Word, which declares that You have plans to prosper me and not to harm me. Help me to see myself the way You see me. In Jesus' name, I pray. Amen."

By accepting and agreeing with God's will for your life, you've taken the first step toward activating His promises. This agreement opens the door for divine guidance, creating the foundation for the next phase of your journey. Now you are ready to take control of your financial destiny.

STEP 2: CAPTURE WHAT'S YOURS

Once you've come into agreement with God's vision for your life, it's time to *seize* what rightfully belongs to you. The enemy has likely taken what is yours, and it's time to take it back. This step is about spiritually reclaiming your financial territory—standing in the authority that God has given you.

Prayer of Seizing: "Father, I come before You as Your daughter, an heir to the Kingdom. I step into my rightful place and reclaim every financial blessing, opportunity, and resource that the enemy has stolen from me and my bloodline. I come into the courts of heaven and I decree and declare that all accusations against me are null and void under the blood of Jesus. I capture every promise You have made to me regarding wealth, prosperity, and inheritance. I take authority over my finances, knowing that I am a rightful owner of all You have prepared for me. In Jesus' mighty name, I reclaim what is mine. Amen."

When you capture what's yours, you are moving in divine authority. Remember, this is not just about claiming money; it's about reclaiming the *right mindset* and *spiritual territory*. The wealth God has for you is tied to your purpose, and when you seize it, you're stepping fully into your Kingdom identity.

STEP 3:
TAKE ACTION NOW

Now is the time to take immediate and decisive action. FFS will attempt to creep back in, telling you that you're not ready, not worthy, or not capable. But that's a lie. The door is open, and God is waiting for you to step through it. It's crucial that you don't delay. When God gives you an assignment, there's a window of opportunity. Moving with urgency shows God that you trust Him and are ready to occupy the territory He's given you.

Prayer of Activation: "Lord, I am ready to take action now. I rebuke the spirit of slothfulness, procrastination, and doubt. I commit to moving in the timing that You have set for me. Every door You have opened, I will walk through without hesitation. Strengthen my faith and resolve so that I do not shrink back. I declare that I am equipped, empowered, and fully able to handle all that You have for me. Lead me in Your perfect timing as I move swiftly to possess the promises You have laid before me. In Jesus' name, I activate my anointing and step into my inheritance. Amen."

This step requires you to act, but not on your own strength. Continue to lean on God for guidance as you take practical steps toward financial freedom. Whether it's launching a business, investing in your financial future, or simply making better money decisions, take action now with the confidence that you are fully equipped to handle the responsibility of ownership.

THIS IS YOUR MOMENT—ACT NOW

If you take nothing else from this journey, remember this: there is an urgency to reclaim what is rightfully yours. You've come too far to hesitate now. The enemy will fight hard, but your anointing and God's power will guide you through. The time for sitting on the sidelines is over.

You've been called to rise up, to move with God, and to reclaim your territory. There will be moments when doubt creeps in. FFS may try to reappear, and the enemy will throw distractions and attacks your way, but God has already declared victory over your life.

Kingdom woman, the time to act is now. You've come too far to allow self-sabotage, doubt, or fear to hold you back any longer. God has already prepared your path, and the door to financial freedom is wide open. Step through it.

Activate your anointing. Reclaim what is rightfully yours. This is your moment—don't let it pass you by.

RIGHTFULLY OWN IT NOW: YOUR PATH FORWARD

Step	Step	Step

Congratulations Video	Claim Your Access	Connect with Our Community

Congratulations!
You are prepared for OWNERSHIP!
I am so proud of you!

If you have read this book, and even re-read this book and begin to apply the information you are starting to see the impact of spiritual and even mental relief from financial restraints.

If you're ready to take these spiritual breakthroughs and turn them into tangible financial success, I have an important message and prayer to activate you for your financial territory!

Take the next step forward and claim what's yours!

1. Resources
2. Financial Wellness Events & Support
3. Access to Me.

It's time to put everything you've learned into action and step fully into the financial freedom God has promised you.

Watch now at www.kiamesheaprewitt.com/privatevideo and take the final step to becoming the rightful owner of your financial destiny.

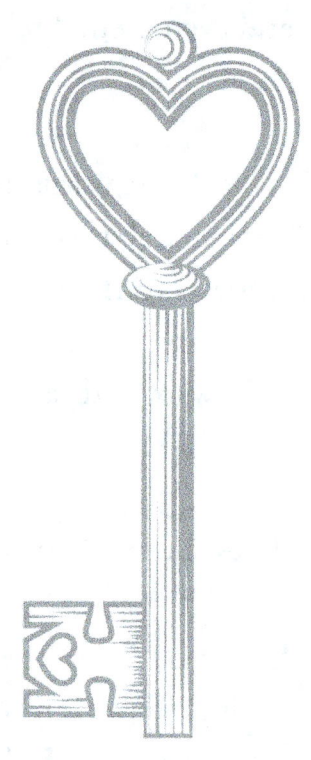

EPILOGUE:

Walking in Ownership

Congratulations! You've completed the journey of *The Rightful Owner*, but this is only the beginning. By now, you've gained deep spiritual insights, dismantled limiting mindsets, and taken bold steps toward reclaiming your financial territory. You've learned to hear God's voice for your finances, to operate in your Kingdom authority, and to activate your anointing.

Now, it's time to **walk in ownership**.

This is the season where you **occupy** and **maintain** your financial territory with urgency and purpose. As you continue to apply these principles, know that challenges may arise, but you are now equipped to face them with the **confidence of a rightful owner**. You've been through the process of deliverance, growth, and refinement. You've been anointed for this assignment, and nothing can take away what God has already ordained for you.

Remember, ownership isn't just a one-time decision—it's a daily walk. **Stay connected to God**, keep your mind and spirit sharp, and surround yourself with the resources and support systems that will help you maintain your momentum.

If you ever need a refresher or a deeper dive into these topics, remember to revisit this book and take advantage of the tools you've learned here. And if you're ready to continue your journey, I encourage you to take the next step and connect with me and follow me on social me at Kiameshea Prewitt on all platforms. Reach out to me, share your feedback about this book, or ask how you can receive even more hands-on guidance to fully occupy your financial inheritance.

You've been called. You've been chosen. And now, you are walking in full authority as the **rightful owner** of your financial destiny.

HIRE KIAMESHEA PREWITT
FOR THE COURAGE TO OWN:
A KINGDOM WOMAN'S
BREAKTHROUGH ACCELERATOR

Step boldly into your God-given identity, birthright, and assignment with the Courage to Own Accelerator. Hire Kiameshea Prewitt today to lead you on a transformative journey that equips high-achieving Kingdom women to fully claim their freedom, purpose, and inheritance.

What is the Courage to Own Accelerator?

The Courage to Own Accelerator is an empowering, breakthrough-driven program designed specifically for women of faith who are ready to rise into their true identity and walk confidently in their God-given assignments. This program combines deep mindset transformation with powerful, actionable breakthroughs that will allow you to shed limiting beliefs, embrace your Kingdom inheritance, and live with the boldness and clarity you were destined for.

Why Kiameshea Prewitt?

Kiameshea Prewitt is dedicated to helping Kingdom women own every aspect of their divine identity and calling. With her deep spiritual wisdom and practical coaching methods, Kiameshea provides the support and tools you need to break free from what's been holding you back and step into a life aligned with God's purpose for you. Her holistic approach ensures that your spiritual growth is matched with real-world progress, allowing you to courageously own your role in the Kingdom.

What You Will Gain:

- ***Identity Ownership:*** Discover the courage to fully own who God has created you to be. This program helps you align your mindset with your divine identity, enabling you to live authentically and purposefully.
- ***Birthright and Assignment Ownership:*** You'll step into your rightful place as a Kingdom woman,

claiming your inheritance and fulfilling your God-given assignment with confidence and authority.

- **Personalized Coaching:** Through one-on-one coaching, Kiameshea will address your unique challenges and guide you through the personalized breakthroughs you need to succeed. Each session is designed to help you fully step into your identity and live out your purpose.

- **Supportive Kingdom Community:** Connect with other like-minded women on the same journey of discovering their true potential. The supportive environment will encourage and uplift you as you walk this path.

Who Should Join?

The Courage to Own Accelerator is for high-achieving Kingdom women who:

- Are ready to break free from limiting beliefs and step into their true God-given identity.
- Desire to own their birthright as daughters of the King and live with boldness, purpose, and confidence.
- Are seeking practical and spiritual guidance to walk fully in their divine assignment.

Expected Outcomes:

By the end of the Courage to Own Accelerator, you will:

- Have the courage and clarity to fully own your identity, birthright, and assignment in the Kingdom.
- Break free from limiting beliefs and mindset barriers that have kept you from your true potential.
- Walk confidently in your God-given purpose, equipped with the tools and strategies to maintain your newfound freedom.

Take the Next Step with Kiameshea Prewitt

If you're ready to step boldly into your Kingdom identity and fulfill your divine assignment, now is the time to hire Kiameshea Prewitt and join the Courage to Own Accelerator. This program is your opportunity to break through limiting beliefs, claim your inheritance, and live with the purpose and freedom you were always meant to have.

SPEAKER FOR HIRE: KIAMESHEA PREWITT

Are you looking for a speaker who will bring lasting transformation and divine insight to your event?

Kiameshea Prewitt is a powerful, anointed speaker, financial coach, and author of *The Rightful Owner*. She specializes in **Kingdom wealth** and **breaking financial strongholds**, combining her compelling personal testimony with years of experience to offer practical, spirit-filled strategies that help women reclaim their financial authority and walk in divine abundance.

Why Book Kiameshea?

With her dynamic and engaging style, Kiameshea is known for delivering impactful messages that leave a lasting impression. Her ability to weave financial expertise with Kingdom principles makes her the perfect speaker for a variety of audiences, whether it's a corporate gathering, women's conference, church retreat, or leadership summit. Kiameshea empowers her listeners to embrace their God-given inheritance and take action to transform their financial lives.

Popular Speaking Topics:

- ***Breaking the 7 Unproductive Money Mindsets***
  Uncover the hidden beliefs that are blocking your financial growth and learn how to break free for good.

- ***Kingdom Wealth: How to Reclaim Your Financial Destiny***
  Discover the principles of Kingdom wealth and how to align your finances with God's divine plan.

- ***The Power of Spiritual Deliverance in Financial Breakthroughs***
  Experience financial freedom by addressing the spiritual roots that may be holding you back.

- ***Stewarding Wealth with Purpose and Authority***
  Learn how to manage your finances with intention and Kingdom authority, aligning your resources with God's purpose.

Bring Kiameshea to Your Next Event

Invite Kiameshea to deliver life-changing insight to your audience. Whether she's speaking on financial breakthroughs or Kingdom wealth principles, her unique blend of spiritual wisdom and financial acumen will inspire and equip your attendees to step into their divine calling.

Book Kiameshea today by visiting Book Kiameshea Now or emailing hello@towerabovefinance.com to inquire about availability and speaking engagements.

Let Kiameshea empower your audience to claim their rightful inheritance and experience financial freedom!

About the Author

Kiameshea Prewitt is a trailblazing **Kingdom Financial Behavioral Specialist**, dedicated to helping high-achieving women break free from limiting financial mindsets and step into their rightful wealth and purpose. As the **discoverer of Financial Fraudulence**—a concept revealing how deeply ingrained beliefs can sabotage financial growth—Kiameshea has made it her mission to empower women to own both their financial and spiritual birthright.

In addition to her groundbreaking work in the financial realm, Kiameshea is the **author of *The Rightful Owner*** and the founder of **TowerAbove Financial Solutions**. Through her work, she provides innovative financial strategies that not only secure wealth but also align with Kingdom principles. Her approach is holistic, addressing the behaviors, mindsets, and spiritual elements that influence financial health.

Kiameshea's **Courage to Own Accelerator** builds on her expertise, equipping women to not only break free from financial limitations but also to claim their God-given inheritance in all areas of life. Her commitment to helping women rise into their divine identity extends beyond finances—she guides them to step fully into their Kingdom assignments with clarity and confidence.

Kiameshea's expertise, coupled with her deep faith and unique insights into financial behavior, have made her a sought-after speaker, coach, and mentor. Through her work, she empowers women to dismantle limiting beliefs, take control of their financial futures, and walk in lasting freedom, both spiritually and financially.

With a passion for helping women claim their full inheritance as daughters of the King, Kiameshea continues to inspire and lead a movement of Kingdom women ready to take ownership of their finances, their purpose, and their destiny.

CONTINUE YOUR JOURNEY WITH KIAMESHEA PREWITT'S BOOKS & RESOURCES

As you dive deeper into your journey of stepping into your identity, purpose, and God-given assignment, why stop here? I invite you to explore more of my resources designed to guide you further into living out your Kingdom inheritance with clarity, intention, and confidence.

The Legacy Blueprint Prayer Journal: God's Plan for Your Money

If you're ready to align your finances with God's divine plan, then **The Legacy Blueprint Prayer Journal: God's Plan For Your Money** is the perfect next step. This journal is more than just a space to write—it's a guided tool designed to help you pray intentionally over your finances, seek God's wisdom, and create a blueprint for building wealth that honors the Kingdom.

Through thought-provoking prompts, scripture-based reflections, and space for personal prayer, this journal helps you partner with God to take control of your financial future. It's time to invite Him into your money decisions and walk confidently in the financial legacy He's designed for you.

Discover More at My Shopify Store

Along with *The Legacy Blueprint Prayer Journal*, my **Shopify store** offers a variety of tools and resources to support you in your spiritual and financial growth. From prayer guides to exclusive coaching materials, you'll find everything you need to continue stepping boldly into your Kingdom calling.

Why Stop Now?

The work you're doing is life-changing, and there are more tools available to help you fully claim your inheritance. Don't miss the opportunity to grow even further with resources tailored to help you break free from financial limitations, walk in spiritual alignment, and fully own your destiny.

Take the Next Step:

- **Purchase** *The Legacy Blueprint Prayer Journal: God's Plan for Your Money* and start transforming your financial life today . https://a.co/d/eJSVFj3

- **Visit my Shopify store** for more empowering tools to continue your journey of faith and freedom.

Your next breakthrough could be just a page away! Ready to go deeper? Head over to my store and see how these resources can support you on your path to true freedom and fulfillment.

www.kiamesheaprewitt.com